DOMME SAYS ...

Published by
BDSM Writers Con, Inc.
PO Box 60985
Staten Island NY 10306

All rights reserved.
ISBN: 978-0-9962731-2-1
Print version
ISBN: 978-0-9962731-3-8
Digital version
Library of Congress Catalog Card Number: Pending

Manufactured in the United States

Email us at: Domme@DommeSays.com

Cover illustration by Kenny Kieman

www.BDSMwriterscon.com

For everyone who dares to desire more!

DOMME SAYS ...

DommeNation ... say it with me!

_____

_____

_____

_____

_____

_____

_____

_____

_____

_____

_____

_____

_____

_____

_____

_____

_____

_____

_____

DOMME SAYS ...

Let me show you all the ways
I plan to use you.

DOMME SAYS ...

Step into my parlor
and discover a new world.

_____

_____

_____

_____

_____

_____

_____

_____

_____

_____

_____

_____

_____

_____

_____

_____

DOMME SAYS ...

I'm not the woman your mother warned you about, I'm the one you've longed for.

DOMME SAYS ...

Fear precedes adventure!

DOMME SAYS ...

I wish everyone practiced submission, then you could gag an idiot when you wanted him to Shut Up!

_____

_____

_____

_____

_____

_____

_____

_____

_____

_____

_____

_____

_____

_____

_____

_____

_____

_____

DOMME SAYS ...

Submission is not debated,
it is shown.

_____
_____
_____
_____
_____

_____
_____
_____
_____
_____
_____
_____
_____
_____
_____
_____
_____
_____

DOMME SAYS ...

Let the decadence shine through!

_____

_____

_____

_____

_____

DOMME SAYS ...

It's the perfect night for a
spanking!

_____

_____

_____

_____

_____

_____

_____

_____

_____

_____

_____

_____

_____

_____

_____

_____

DOMME SAYS...

There is never a time limit on
submission, but there is a time
limit on my patience.

DOMME SAYS ...

Submission, you either give it
or you don't.

_____

_____

_____

_____

_____

_____

_____

_____

_____

_____

_____

_____

_____

_____

_____

_____

_____

_____

DOMME SAYS ...

Practice RACK
Risk Aware Consensual Kink

_____

_____

_____

_____

_____

DOMME SAYS ...

When I said size doesn't matter,
I was only joking!

_____

_____

_____

_____

_____

_____

_____

_____

_____

_____

_____

_____

_____

_____

_____

_____

_____

DOMME SAYS …

Roses are red, violets are blue,
I'm going to tie you up
and do naughty things to you.

_____

_____

_____

_____

_____

_____

_____

_____

_____

_____

_____

_____

_____

_____

_____

_____

DOMME SAYS ...

To the wrong person, you'll never
have any worth. To me, you'll
mean everything!

_____

_____

_____

_____

_____

_____

_____

_____

_____

_____

_____

_____

_____

_____

_____

_____

_____

DOMME SAYS …

Boys make good pets … but a
man makes me growl …
mmmm…

_____

_____

_____

_____

DOMME SAYS ...

Just a little bit of rope
makes the world go round.

_____

_____

_____

_____

_____

_____

_____

_____

_____

_____

_____

_____

_____

_____

_____

_____

_____

_____

_____

_____

DOMME SAYS ...

He won't run away;
he's tied up in the den.

_____
_____
_____
_____
_____

_____
_____
_____
_____
_____
_____
_____
_____
_____
_____
_____
_____

DOMME SAYS ...

Cooking cuffs,
the perfect gift for any slave.

_____

_____

_____

_____

_____

_____

_____

_____

_____

_____

_____

_____

_____

_____

_____

_____

_____

_____

DOMME SAYS ...

Some days it's not worth
chewing through the leather straps
in the morning.

_____

_____

_____

_____

DOMME SAYS ...

Mediocrity is not accepted here!

DOMME SAYS ...

I don't bite ... much!

_____

_____

_____

_____

_____

DOMME SAYS ...

Failure is not an option,
but spankings and floggings are!

_____

_____

_____

_____

_____

DOMME SAYS ...

Have a Spankalicious Day!

_____

_____

_____

_____

_____

_____

_____

_____

_____

_____

_____

_____

_____

_____

_____

_____

_____

_____

DOMME SAYS ...

When I look at you, I think of all
the ways I want to tie you up.
Ssssh ... I'm counting!

_____

_____

_____

_____

_____

_____

_____

_____

_____

_____

_____

_____

_____

_____

_____

_____

_____

DOMME SAYS ...

Things to pick up at the market:
clothespins, clamps, rope ...

DOMME SAYS ...

Surrender and let me play!

_____

_____

_____

_____

_____

_____

_____

_____

_____

_____

_____

_____

_____

_____

_____

_____

_____

_____

_____

DOMME SAYS ...

Men ... every woman
should own one!

_____

_____

_____

_____

_____

_____

_____

_____

_____

_____

_____

_____

_____

_____

_____

_____

_____

DOMME SAYS ...

I love men with long hair.
It makes it easier to drag their
face where I want it.

_____

_____

_____

_____

_____

_____

_____

_____

_____

_____

_____

_____

_____

_____

_____

_____

_____

DOMME SAYS ...

Oh dear, I think I've caused
an owwie. Let me kiss it
and make it better.

_____
_____
_____
_____

_____
_____
_____
_____
_____
_____
_____
_____
_____
_____
_____

DOMME SAYS ...

Blindfolds anyone?

_____

_____

_____

_____

_____

DOMME SAYS ...

Don't think of it as punishment;
think of it as
character development.

_____
_____
_____
_____

DOMME SAYS ...

Floggings and spankings
are an excellent form of exercise.
Perform them daily!

_____

_____

_____

_____

_____

_____

_____

_____

_____

_____

_____

_____

_____

_____

_____

DOMME SAYS ...

Practice being sensual in
EVERYTHING you do!

_____

_____

_____

_____

_____

_____

_____

_____

_____

_____

_____

_____

_____

_____

_____

_____

_____

_____

DOMME SAYS ...

Dominance is not a role I play,
it is who *I am.*

_____

_____

_____

_____

_____

_____

_____

_____

_____

_____

_____

_____

_____

_____

_____

_____

_____

_____

_____

_____

_____

_____

DOMME SAYS ...

Don't just throw yourself at my
feet, I hate it when I trip over you.

_____

_____

_____

_____

_____

_____

_____

_____

_____

_____

_____

_____

_____

_____

_____

_____

_____

_____

_____

DOMME SAYS...

How about I light up your world
with a little Fire Play?

_____

_____

_____

_____

_____

DOMME SAYS ...

Complacency ...
is a fool's drug of choice!

DOMME SAYS ...

If you break your toys you won't
have anyone to play with.

_____

_____

_____

_____

_____

_____

_____

_____

_____

_____

_____

_____

_____

_____

_____

_____

_____

DOMME SAYS ...

Start the day off right. Jot down all the naughty things you wish to try and then go out and do them.

_____

_____

_____

_____

_____

_____

_____

_____

_____

_____

_____

_____

_____

_____

_____

_____

_____

_____

DOMME SAYS ...

All you need is a little chocolate,
your favorite shoes, and a dash of
pleasure and pain.

_____

_____

_____

_____

_____

_____

_____

_____

_____

_____

_____

_____

_____

_____

_____

_____

DOMME SAYS ...

Dominance is like breathing.
You either do it or
you shrivel up and die.

_____

_____

_____

_____

DOMME SAYS ...

1 ... 2 ... 3 ...
Come on, count with me!

_____
_____
_____
_____
_____

_____
_____
_____
_____
_____
_____
_____
_____
_____
_____
_____
_____
_____
_____

DOMME SAYS ...

Floggers, rope, and whips
oh my!

_____

_____

_____

_____

_____

DOMME SAYS ...

I don't hate men,
I merely love them more
when they beg and scream.

DOMME SAYS ...

You want to be my worm?
Do I look like someone
who likes fishing?

_____

_____

_____

_____

_____

_____

_____

_____

_____

_____

_____

_____

_____

_____

_____

_____

_____

DOMME SAYS ...

Ruin or rapture?
Which one would you
prefer today?

_____

_____

_____

_____

_____

_____

_____

_____

_____

_____

_____

_____

_____

_____

_____

_____

_____

_____

DOMME SAYS ...

All I want is a few good men!

_____

_____

_____

_____

_____

_____

_____

_____

_____

_____

_____

_____

_____

_____

_____

_____

_____

_____

DOMME SAYS ...

If you want to be a great
Dominant, start by controlling
yourself first.

DOMME SAYS ...

The path isn't always smooth;
sometimes you trip over
a slave or two.

_____

_____

_____

_____

_____

_____

_____

_____

_____

_____

_____

_____

_____

_____

_____

_____

_____

_____

_____

DOMME SAYS ...

If you really want to punish
your submissive, tie them up and
stick them in a corner. Then have
fun with a friend.

_____

_____

_____

_____

_____

_____

_____

_____

_____

_____

_____

_____

_____

_____

_____

_____

DOMME SAYS ...

Duct tape is a gal's best friend!

_____

_____

_____

_____

_____

DOMME SAYS ...

It's perfectly ok to love them, tie
them up, and paddle their butt.
They'll thank you for it!

_____

_____

_____

_____

_____

_____

_____

_____

_____

_____

_____

_____

_____

_____

_____

_____

DOMME SAYS ...

Spank 'em and whip 'em;
they'll love you for it.

_____

_____

_____

_____

_____

_____

_____

_____

_____

_____

_____

_____

_____

_____

_____

_____

_____

_____

_____

_____

DOMME SAYS ...

One-night stands are great because in the morning you can knock on their door and start all over again.

_____

_____

_____

_____

_____

_____

_____

_____

_____

_____

_____

_____

_____

_____

_____

_____

_____

DOMME SAYS ...

Tying your lover to the wall gives a whole new meaning to the term "Wall Art!"

_____

_____

_____

_____

_____

_____

_____

_____

_____

_____

_____

_____

_____

_____

_____

_____

_____

DOMME SAYS ...

Some gals like chocolate, but give
this Domme a whip every time!

_____

_____

_____

_____

_____

_____

_____

_____

_____

_____

_____

_____

_____

_____

_____

_____

_____

_____

DOMME SAYS ...

Give me a little rope
and I'll tie you up with it.

_____

_____

_____

_____

_____

_____

_____

_____

_____

_____

_____

_____

_____

_____

_____

_____

_____

_____

Girls like shoes. Dommes prefer
floggers, whips, leather and lace.

Domme Says ...

DOMME SAYS ...

Girls like shoes. Dommes prefer floggers, whips, leather and lace.

DOMME SAYS ...

Save a horse, ride a slave!

_____

_____

_____

_____

_____

DOMME SAYS ...

Hard limits are for … everyone!
chuckles
What did you think
I was going to say?

_____

_____

_____

_____

_____

_____

_____

_____

_____

_____

_____

_____

_____

_____

_____

_____

_____

_____

DOMME SAYS ...

A spanking a day
keeps bad behavior at bay.

_____

_____

_____

_____

_____

_____

_____

_____

_____

_____

_____

_____

_____

_____

_____

_____

_____

_____

_____

DOMME SAYS ...

I love marking my slave

DOMME SAYS...

If you want someone trained right, you have to be willing to teach, correct, and then teach them again.

DOMME SAYS ...

Protocols and Rituals
are essential for a healthy
BDSM relationship.

_____

_____

_____

_____

_____

_____

_____

_____

_____

_____

_____

_____

_____

_____

_____

_____

DOMME SAYS ...

Forget the roses.
Give me a violet wand
and an electrical socket.

_____
_____
_____
_____

_____
_____
_____
_____
_____
_____
_____
_____
_____
_____
_____
_____
_____

DOMME SAYS ...

I'm not a pervert, I merely
embrace life and love in all
its primal beauty.

_____

_____

_____

_____

_____

_____

_____

_____

_____

_____

_____

_____

_____

_____

_____

_____

DOMME SAYS ...

If you love someone set them free. When they come back to you, chain them to the railing.

_____

_____

_____

_____

_____

_____

_____

_____

_____

_____

_____

_____

_____

_____

_____

_____

_____

_____

DOMME SAYS ...

Meet me at BDSM Writers Con,
I'll be the one in the front row.

_____

_____

_____

_____

_____

_____

_____

_____

_____

_____

_____

_____

_____

_____

_____

_____

_____

_____

DOMME SAYS ...

I'm easy to please. I merely
require that you give me your all.

_____

_____

_____

_____

_____

_____

_____

_____

_____

_____

_____

_____

_____

_____

_____

_____

_____

_____

_____

DOMME SAYS ...

Be impeccable with your D/s.

_____

_____

_____

_____

_____

_____

_____

_____

_____

_____

_____

_____

_____

_____

_____

_____

_____

_____

DOMME SAYS ...

If you want to make your
Domme's heart soar,
offer her your true submission.

_____

_____

_____

_____

_____

_____

_____

_____

_____

_____

_____

_____

_____

_____

_____

DOMME SAYS ...

BDSM is a world where you put
your emotional & physical life on
the line. There is no room for lies!

_____

_____

_____

_____

_____

_____

_____

_____

_____

_____

_____

_____

_____

_____

_____

_____

_____

DOMME SAYS ...

Live, love and do not fear
pain ... well ok, just a little.

_____

_____

_____

_____

_____

_____

_____

_____

_____

_____

_____

_____

_____

_____

_____

_____

_____

_____

DOMME SAYS ...

It's not "topping from the bottom"
   if you tell me what you like.
   You're merely being helpful.

DOMME SAYS...

It hurts so good you'll love it!

_____

_____

_____

_____

_____

_____

_____

_____

_____

_____

_____

_____

_____

_____

_____

_____

_____

_____

_____

DOMME SAYS ...

I love a man who's well educated.
It's fun to hear them babble.

_____

_____

_____

_____

_____

_____

_____

_____

_____

_____

_____

_____

_____

_____

_____

_____

_____

DOMME SAYS ...

Red. Yellow. Green.
It's not just for traffic lights.

DOMME SAYS ...

Communication is oh so sexy!

_____
_____
_____
_____
_____

_____
_____
_____
_____
_____
_____
_____
_____
_____
_____
_____
_____

DOMME SAYS …

When in doubt think,
"WWMDW?"
(What would my *Domme* want?)

_____

_____

_____

_____

_____

_____

_____

_____

_____

_____

_____

_____

_____

_____

_____

_____

_____

Domme Says ...

DOMME SAYS ...

The correct answer is,
"Yes, Ma'am."

DOMME SAYS...

Nothing annoys me more than a
submissive with a grocery list of
things he wants me to do
when we've just met.

_____

_____

_____

_____

_____

_____

_____

_____

_____

_____

_____

_____

_____

_____

_____

DOMME SAYS ...

Just because you tell me
what you want, doesn't mean
I'm going to give it to you.

_____

_____

_____

_____

_____

_____

_____

_____

_____

_____

_____

_____

_____

_____

_____

_____

DOMME SAYS ...

Mind F**ks ... color me happy!

_____

_____

_____

_____

_____

_____

_____

_____

_____

_____

_____

_____

_____

_____

_____

_____

_____

_____

_____

DOMME SAYS ...

When you're happy
and you know it ... scream!

_____

_____

_____

_____

_____

_____

_____

_____

_____

_____

_____

_____

_____

_____

_____

_____

_____

_____

_____

DOMME SAYS ...

What do hickies and spankings
have in common?
They both leave my mark behind!

DOMME SAYS ...

I love presents;
both receiving and giving.

_____
_____
_____
_____
_____

_____
_____
_____
_____
_____
_____
_____
_____
_____
_____
_____
_____
_____

Dr. Charley Ferrer

DOMME SAYS …

Watching a slave surrender is like seeing the sunset for the first time.

_____
_____
_____
_____
_____

_____
_____
_____
_____
_____
_____
_____
_____
_____
_____

DOMME SAYS...

Submission is only a treasure
when it's given freely.

_____

_____

_____

_____

_____

DOMME SAYS ...

Practice random acts of kindness,
give someone a BDSM book.

_____

_____

_____

_____

_____

DOMME SAYS ...

It's ok to be a little nervous. It
makes tormenting you more fun.

_____

_____

_____

_____

_____

_____

_____

_____

_____

_____

_____

_____

_____

_____

_____

_____

_____

_____

_____

_____

_____

DOMME SAYS ...

No ... Don't ... Stop...
are *NOT* safewords!

_____

_____

_____

_____

_____

_____

_____

_____

_____

_____

_____

_____

_____

_____

_____

_____

_____

_____

_____

DOMME SAYS ...

Just because you've had enough
doesn't mean we're finished.

_____

_____

_____

_____

_____

_____

_____

_____

_____

_____

_____

_____

_____

_____

_____

_____

DOMME SAYS ...

Communication is not an option;
it's a requirement!

_____

_____

_____

_____

_____

_____

_____

_____

_____

_____

_____

_____

_____

_____

_____

_____

DOMME SAYS ...

You are never more beautiful than
when you are submitting to me!

DOMME SAYS...

Well? It's not going to lick itself!

_____

_____

_____

_____

_____

_____

_____

_____

_____

_____

_____

_____

_____

_____

_____

_____

_____

_____

_____

DOMME SAYS ...

Spankalicious ...
that should be an ice cream flavor.

_____

_____

_____

_____

_____

DOMME SAYS ...

If you tell me what you want,
there's a 50/50 chance
I'll do it for you.

_____

_____

_____

_____

_____

_____

_____

_____

_____

_____

_____

_____

_____

_____

_____

_____

_____

_____

_____

DOMME SAYS ...

BDSM is a healthy way
to express your love and desire
for another person.

_____

_____

_____

_____

_____

_____

_____

_____

_____

_____

_____

_____

_____

_____

_____

_____

DOMME SAYS ...

BDSM is about HOW
you love and show affection.

DOMME SAYS ...

slaves and submissives ...
need I say more?

_____

_____

_____

_____

_____

_____

_____

_____

_____

_____

_____

_____

_____

_____

_____

_____

_____

_____

DOMME SAYS ...

It's better to have loved and lost
than live with a psycho!

_____

_____

_____

_____

_____

_____

_____

_____

_____

_____

_____

_____

_____

_____

_____

_____

_____

DOMME SAYS ...

I'm not here to perform for you
or service your needs.
That's your job.

_____
_____
_____
_____

DOMME SAYS ...

Dominance … it's my special way
of interacting.

_____

_____

_____

_____

_____

_____

_____

_____

_____

_____

_____

_____

_____

_____

_____

_____

_____

_____

_____

_____

DOMME SAYS ...

To love me is to worship me!

_____

_____

_____

_____

_____

_____

_____

_____

_____

_____

_____

_____

_____

_____

_____

_____

_____

_____

DOMME SAYS ...

Just because I love being in charge, doesn't mean I don't want a man to sweep me off my feet.

_____

_____

_____

_____

_____

_____

_____

_____

_____

_____

_____

_____

_____

_____

_____

_____

DOMME SAYS ...

Safe. Sane. Consensual.
They're not just words to say,
they are words to live by.

_____

_____

_____

_____

_____

_____

_____

_____

_____

_____

_____

_____

_____

_____

_____

_____

_____

DOMME SAYS ...

BDSM requires much of you.
Your integrity, trust, honesty and
willingness to surrender ALL
to each other.

DOMME SAYS ...

Turn toward me when you're
scared, not away.

_____

_____

_____

_____

_____

DOMME SAYS ...

Trust isn't merely what a
submissive needs from
their Dominant. It's what a
Dominant needs from their
submissive as well.

_____

_____

_____

_____

_____

_____

_____

_____

_____

_____

_____

_____

_____

_____

_____

_____

DOMME SAYS ...

Always do your research.

DOMME SAYS …

Safe sex is something to consider
whether you're vanilla or D/s.

_____

_____

_____

_____

_____

_____

_____

_____

_____

_____

_____

_____

_____

_____

_____

_____

_____

DOMME SAYS ...

Start your day off right;
spank your slave!

_____

_____

_____

_____

_____

DOMME SAYS...

RACK. It's what I live by.
This way you know it's going to
hurt before we get started.

_____
_____
_____
_____

_____
_____
_____
_____
_____
_____
_____
_____
_____
_____
_____
_____
_____
_____

DOMME SAYS...

Just because you're not able or
willing to submit, does not mean
I'm not able to dominate.

_____
_____
_____
_____

_____
_____
_____
_____
_____
_____
_____
_____
_____
_____
_____
_____
_____

DOMME SAYS ...

You make me tingle all over when
you kneel before me.

_____

_____

_____

_____

_____

DOMME SAYS ...

It's like they always say,
"If you want to be great at
something, practice, practice,
PRACTICE!

_____

_____

_____

_____

_____

_____

_____

_____

_____

_____

_____

_____

_____

_____

_____

_____

_____

DOMME SAYS ...

Pain = Pleasure
Pleasure = Pain
It really is simply to remember!

_____

_____

_____

_____

DOMME SAYS ...

It's not all whips and chains;
I like to cuddle too.

_____

_____

_____

_____

_____

_____

_____

_____

_____

_____

_____

_____

_____

_____

_____

_____

_____

_____

DOMME SAYS …

Cooking and cleaning
is not just for women …
male submissives like it too!

_____
_____
_____
_____

_____
_____
_____
_____
_____
_____
_____
_____
_____
_____
_____
_____
_____
_____
_____

DOMME SAYS ...

Who's the bitch now?

_____

_____

_____

_____

_____

_____

_____

_____

_____

_____

_____

_____

_____

_____

_____

_____

_____

_____

DOMME SAYS …

Not sure what to tell vanilla
friends when they ask what you're
doing? Repeat after me,
"I'm doing research!"

_____

_____

_____

_____

DOMME SAYS...

I love making you mine!

_____

_____

_____

_____

_____

DOMME SAYS ...

Did that hurt?
I didn't feel a thing.

_____
_____
_____
_____
_____

_____
_____
_____
_____
_____
_____
_____
_____
_____
_____
_____
_____

DOMME SAYS...

If you like exploring, this lifestyle
will take you to amazing places
you've never seen before.

_____

_____

_____

_____

_____

_____

_____

_____

_____

_____

_____

_____

_____

_____

_____

_____

DOMME SAYS ...

When I was a child, I loved to play with toys. Nope, I never lost the taste for it.

Domme Says ....

DOMME SAYS ...

I love music. It helps me keep my
rhythm when I'm flogging.

_____

_____

_____

_____

_____

_____

_____

_____

_____

_____

_____

_____

_____

_____

_____

_____

_____

_____

DOMME SAYS ...

BDSM isn't a phase I'm going through, it's what calls to my soul.

_____

_____

_____

_____

_____

_____

_____

_____

_____

_____

_____

_____

_____

_____

_____

_____

_____

_____

_____

DOMME SAYS ...

The sexiest thing I've ever seen
on a man was my collar
around his throat.

_____

_____

_____

_____

_____

_____

_____

_____

_____

_____

_____

_____

_____

_____

_____

_____

DOMME SAYS ...

I'm just a little bit sadistic.

_____

_____

_____

_____

_____

_____

_____

_____

_____

_____

_____

_____

_____

_____

_____

_____

_____

_____

_____

DOMME SAYS ...

Oh poor baby,
let me kiss the boo-boo.

_____
_____
_____
_____
_____

_____
_____
_____
_____
_____
_____
_____
_____
_____
_____
_____
_____
_____

DOMME SAYS...

When I think about you,
I stroke my cat-o-nine tails.

_____

_____

_____

_____

_____

_____

_____

_____

_____

_____

_____

_____

_____

_____

_____

_____

_____

_____

_____

DOMME SAYS ...

Can I keep you?

_____

_____

_____

_____

_____

DOMME SAYS...

If you let me tie you up, you can touch me all you want.

DOMME SAYS...

Mama always said,
"If you want to keep a man,
tie him to your bed."

_____

_____

_____

_____

_____

_____

_____

_____

_____

_____

_____

_____

_____

_____

_____

_____

_____

DOMME SAYS ...

I'm not broken,
nor do I need to be fixed.
I'm perfect just the way I am!

_____

_____

_____

_____

_____

_____

_____

_____

_____

_____

_____

_____

_____

_____

_____

_____

_____

DOMME SAYS ...

Don't believe everything you read about this lifestyle. Do your own research and learn the truths.

_____

_____

_____

_____

_____

_____

_____

_____

_____

_____

_____

_____

_____

_____

_____

DOMME SAYS ...

BDSM is not domestic violence.
Learn the difference.

_____
_____
_____
_____
_____
_____
_____
_____
_____
_____
_____
_____
_____
_____
_____
_____
_____
_____
_____
_____
_____

DOMME SAYS ...

BDSM isn't about how you look
on the outside, it's about who
you are on the inside.

_____

_____

_____

_____

_____

_____

_____

_____

_____

_____

_____

_____

_____

_____

_____

_____

_____

DOMME SAYS ...

Roleplaying online may be fun,
but to really understand
dominance and submission
you have to actually do it.

_____

_____

_____

_____

_____

_____

_____

_____

_____

_____

_____

_____

_____

_____

_____

_____

_____

DOMME SAYS ...

Always have a safety call when
meeting someone in private.

_____

_____

_____

_____

_____

_____

_____

_____

_____

_____

_____

_____

_____

_____

_____

_____

_____

DOMME SAYS...

BDSM is not about malice nor
pride, it's about sharing a sacred
part of yourself with another.

_____

_____

_____

_____

_____

_____

_____

_____

_____

_____

_____

_____

_____

_____

_____

_____

_____

DOMME SAYS ...

DommeNation…say it with me!

_____

_____

_____

_____

_____

_____

_____

_____

_____

_____

_____

_____

_____

_____

_____

_____

_____

_____

Curious about Dominance and submission?

Then join us for our next BDSM Writers Con held annually in New York City and Everett, Washington.

BDSM Writers Con is the only conference dedicated to teaching writers and readers about the extraordinary world of Dominance and submission. Our one-of-a-kink conference has over 30 hours of workshops and live demonstrations on BDSM, plus we host the prestigious Golden Flogger Award ceremonies and various Mix and Mingles. There's even a trip to a private BDSM Club party. We end each conference with a BDSM Book Fair and Fetish Vending event.

We host the only BDSM Writers Ball, in Everett, Washington and the prestigious Golden Flogger Award ceremony in New York City.

BDSM Writers Con is unlike any other conference! We've been called the gateway for authors and readers into the world of Dominance and submission. We are the definitive conference for anyone interested in this unique genre.

Join us and discover for yourself why participants return year after year!

BDSM Writers Con was founded by Dr. Charley Ferrer, world-renowned Clinical Sexologist and America's Intimacy and BDSM Educator.

www.BDSMWritersCon.com

Dr. Charley Ferrer is the award-winning author of over fourteen books on sexuality and self-empowerment including her international bestselling book BDSM The Naked Truth, which provides valuable information on various aspects of the power exchange. Doctor Charley is the founder of BDSM Writers Con, the definitive conference for anyone interested in writing about or exploring the world of Dominance and submission. Other books and resources by her Dr. Charley Ferrer:

BDSM The Naked Truth
BDSM for Writers
Domme Says Journal Book
Sex Unlimited
The Latina Kama Sutra
The W.I.S.E. Journal for the Sensual Woman

Anthologies
BDSM Writers Con Anthology 2015
First Annual BDSM Writers Con 2014
Yin Rising

Audio Programs
BDSM Intensive

Websites

www.DommeSays.com

www.BDSMTheNakedTruth.com

www.BDSMWritersCon.com

www.DoctorCharley.com

www.ingramcontent.com/pod-product-compliance
Lightning Source LLC
Chambersburg PA
CBHW061728020426
42331CB00006B/1143